Jessica Caws is a financial services regulatory specialist. She leads the financial services regulatory practice and is co-head of financial services at a Top 50 UK law firm. Prior to her current role she trained at and subsequently spent 10 years working at an international law firm headquartered in London. At the time of writing Jessica had 12 years of post-qualification experience advising on financial services regulation. Advising on the regulatory perimeter is one of Jessica's specialist areas of expertise.

A Practical Guide to Perimeter Guidance on Regulated Activities (PERG)

A Practical Guide to Perimeter Guidance on Regulated Activities (PERG)

Jessica Caws
MA, LLB (Hons)

Law Brief Publishing

Published 2025 by Law Brief Publishing, an imprint of Law Brief Publishing Ltd
30 The Parks
Minehead
Somerset
TA24 8BT

www.lawbriefpublishing.com

Paperback: 978-1-916698-95-6

CONTENTS

CHAPTER ONE

INTRODUCTION

1.1 Interpreting UK financial services legislation can be a frustrating task. The drafting can sometimes be unclear, while the relevant sections are not always immediately obvious. This is due to many years of amendments to the law, largely linked to the implementation of European legislation which has in many cases been imposed on top of the UK's existing regulatory framework. Policy and political changes (in particular, Brexit), have also led to further amendments. The result is a network of regulation that to the uninitiated can be daunting to review.

1.2 The FCA's perimeter guidance manual (which I shall refer to throughout this book as PERG) is one of regulatory lawyers' favourite sectors of the FCA Handbook. It is written in a (relatively) clear and simple way and gives clarity to some of the more confusing elements of the regulatory framework. It is a great companion to those who are looking to understand what sits within the FCA's regulatory remit, as the boundary as to what is caught is not always clear cut.

1.3 The purpose of this guide is to give the reader some additional pointers on navigating PERG. The guide aims to point to the most useful sections and also to highlight interesting or quirky points. Sometimes it is not clear that certain sections of PERG may be useful to your analysis and I will also point these out.

1.4 A point on scoping

1.4.1 This guide will focus on areas of common interest rather than specialist sub-categories such as regulated lending (which is an area which could do with its own "practical guide"!).

1.4.2 The purpose of this guide is to focus on the key regulated activities, those ordinarily understood to be "investment business", as well as giving an overview of the regulatory framework that applies.

1.4.3 For the avoidance of doubt, this guide will not cover the following in detail;

1.4.3.1 Insurance and insurance distribution;

1.4.3.2 Debt adjusting type activities;

1.4.3.3 Consumer credit and home finance activities;

1.4.3.4 Activities relating to investment funds such as the activities relating to operating collective investment schemes and managing alternative investment funds;

1.4.3.5 Electronic money and payment services.

1.4.4 The intention of this guide is to focus on regulated activities. Of course, one of the other key regimes in relation to the UK financial services framework is the financial promotion regime. Please see the defined term "Financial Promotion" for more information.

1.5 A note on MiFID

1.5.1 When the UK was part of Europe, European financial services legislation needed to be reflected in our regime. It was generally considered that the UK position "gold plated" the European regime, so instead of replacing the UK framework, European legislation was somewhat laid on top of it. This is very much the case with MiFID, which is the European legislation that applies to investment firms.

1.5.2 This guide will not consider MiFID in detail, however it will make reference to MiFID when it is specifically relevant, for example in relation to overrides. Other European regimes such as the Alternative Investment Fund Managers Directive are outside scope of this guide.

1.6 I hope that you find PERG as helpful as I do in interpreting the trickier areas of the web of UK financial services legislation and that this guide aids in your navigation of PERG.

1.7 Of course, do not take as conclusive or rely on any of the information set out in this guide; it gives some views on interpretation based on experience, but you must make your own assessment and draw your own conclusions. Any views expressed are my own and do not represent the views of the FCA.

1.8 The law described in this book is believed to be accurate at 30th July 2025. As financial services legislation changes regularly, it is advisable to check the up-to-date regulatory material.

CHAPTER TWO

DEFINED TERMS

2.1 It is often said about financial services lawyers that we love acronyms. When we present to or even communicate with other lawyers we are known to speak a language unique to FS Reg lawyers: COBS, OEICs, AIFs.... The list goes on!

2.2 To assist with interpretation of FS jargon, I have set out below some of the defined terms / acronyms that will be used throughout this guide for your reference:

AIF: means an alternative investment fund;

Business Order: means the FSMA (Carrying on Regulated Activities by Way of Business) Order 2001;

CIS: means the FSMA (Collective Investment Schemes Order) 2001;

CIS Order: means Financial Services and Markets Act 2000 (Collective Investment Schemes Order) 2001;

Contractually based investments: means in accordance with Article 3(1) of the RAO, options, futures, contracts for differences (and rights to or interests in these types of investments). There are also other types of contracts that fall within this definition that are not the subject of this guide;

FCA: means the Financial Conduct Authority, or any successor entity;

Financial Promotion: means an invitation or inducement communicated in the course of business to engage in investment activity. It is a criminal offence pursuant to Section 21 of FSMA to make a Financial Promotion without being authorised under FSMA, unless a relevant exemption applies (the **Financial Promotion Restriction**). The exemptions applying are set out in the FPO;

FPO: means the FSMA (Financial Promotion) Order 2005;

FSMA: means the Financial Services and Markets Act 2000;

General Prohibition: means the restriction on carrying on of regulated activities set out in Section 19 of FSMA;

Investment Services: means the list of investment services under MiFID (Section A of Annex 1 of MiFID now onshored in Part 3 of Schedule 2 of the RAO);

MiFID: means Directive 2014/65/EU of the European Parliament and of the Council of 15 May 2014 on markets in financial instruments;

MiFID investment firm: a firm to which MiFID would apply if it had its head office or registered office in the EEA. This includes investment firms (persons whose regular occupation or business is the provision of one or more Investment Services to third parties and/or the performance of these on a professional basis) with their head offices in the UK;

OEIC: means open-ended investment company;

PERG: means the FCA's perimeter guidance manual;

RAO: means the FSMA (Regulated Activities Order) 2001;

Securities: means the investments listed out at Article 3(1) of the RAO, and includes investments like shares, debentures, warrants, units in funds etc;

UCITS: means undertakings for collective investment in transferable securities (a type of retail fund).

2.3 You should also be aware that there is a comprehensive Glossary as part of the FCA Handbook where you can look up any financial services term and be able to find its definition.

CHAPTER THREE

WHAT IS PERG?

3.1 PERG is the acronym given to the FCA's Perimeter Guidance Manual, which is where the FCA sets out its guidance on the scope of the "regulatory perimeter". In other words, this is what sits within the remit of the FCA's oversight and what does not.

3.2 Status of guidance under PERG

3.3 It is important to make clear the status of the guidance in PERG as this gives you an indication of the extent to which you can rely on it in your analysis.

3.4 The FCA states at PERG 1.3.1 G (G standing for guidance) that the guidance set out in PERG represents the FCA's view on certain matters and that if a person follows PERG, the FCA will take the view that the person has complied with the aspects of the requirement to which the guidance relates.

3.5 In other words, if you follow PERG, you should be comfortable that you are acting in accordance with the regulatory position in the eyes of the FCA. However, the point should be made that there may be other ways to be compliant that do not fall strictly within PERG. Nevertheless, it is always a good idea to fall within PERG if at all possible to avoid sitting within an area of uncertainty.

3.6 Further, the FCA makes the point that PERG does not bind the courts (although FCA rules (labelled with an R) will do). However, the FCA confirms that PERG may be of "persuasive effect" if making an argument to the courts. It is often the case that the courts will take FCA guidance into account however, as it can be helpful to decision-making.

CHAPTER FOUR

THE REGULATORY FRAMEWORK FOR REGULATED ACTIVITIES

4.1 The general prohibition

4.2 This guide focusses on perimeter guidance related to *regulated activities* in relation to *investment business*. Set out below are the key regulatory provisions to be aware of in relation to the carrying on of regulated activities in the UK.

4.3 Our "golden rule" in financial services is found at Section 19 of FSMA, otherwise known as the General Prohibition. This rule confirms that no person may carry on a regulated activity in the UK unless they are authorised by the FCA with Part 4A FSMA permission to do so, or they are an "exempt person".

4.4 Section 23 of FSMA confirms that it is in fact a criminal offence if a person carries on regulated activities in breach of the General Prohibition. The penalties for breach of the General Prohibition include imprisonment and an unlimited fine.

4.5 While the criminal implications alone should be enough to deter people from carrying on regulated activities without authorisation, Section 26 to 29 of FSMA confirm that agreements entered into as a result of the carrying on of such regulated activities in breach of the General Prohibition may be unenforceable.

4.6 In other words, a lender may not be able to take enforcement action to recover monies lent under a loan agreement where this should have been treated as a regulated credit agreement. Or someone who invests in an unlisted company may claim that the subscription agreement is unenforceable, which means that they are entitled to the return of their original investment. I have found that the commercial consequences of breach of the General Prohibition can often be more persuasive in real terms to clients.

4.7 It is both the criminal and practical consequences of breach of the General Prohibition that make it essential to establish whether an exemption or exclusion exists or whether it is necessary to become authorised directly by the FCA (or make use of an appointed representative arrangement, where a person shelters under the regulatory umbrella of an authorised firm).

4.8 The regulated activities and any relevant exemptions that are available are set out in the FSMA (Regulated Activities) Order 2001, otherwise known as the RAO. Information on regulated activities and exclusions is set out in Part 6.

4.9 **The business element**

4.9.1 Section 22 of FSMA makes clear that for an activity to be a regulated activity, it must be carried on "by way of business".

4.9.2 PERG 2.3.2 G confirms that HM Treasury has exercised a power pursuant to FSMA to change the meaning of the above "business element" (see the Business Order). What this means is that the business element actually differs depending on the type of regulated activity that is carried on. This is explored below.

4.9.3 The FSMA Test

4.9.3.1 The general FSMA test for certain regulated activities confirms that these must be carried on "by way of business" (the **FSMA Test**).

4.9.3.2 PERG helpfully explains at PERG 2.3.2 G (4) that this applies to the key activities of:

(a) Effecting or carrying out contracts of insurance;

(b) Entering into or administering a home finance transaction;

(c) Credit related regulated activities (note that this is modified in part in relation to not for profit bodies but only in relation to the activities of debt adjusting or providing credit information services (this is interesting, as it implies that not for profit bodies can in the FCA's view carry on regulated activities by way of business. This probably captures the activities of charities that charge fees, for example independent schools. Nevertheless it can be frustrating for charity clients that they are not entirely carved out from the carrying on of regulated activities); and

(d) Operating an electronic system in relation to lending.

4.9.3.3 There is very helpful guidance set out in PERG at 2.3.3 G to the effect that whether or not an activity is carried on "by way of business" is ultimately a question of judgment that takes account of several factors. Crucially, none of which of these factors are likely to be conclusive and all of these must be considered together, bearing in mind the relevant facts. The FCA lists these as:

(a) The degree of continuity of the activity carried on;

(b) The existence of a commercial element;

(c) The scale of the activity; and

(d) The proportion which the activity bears to other activities carried on by the same person but which are not regulated.

4.9.3.4 Question 38D of PERG 14.5 tells us that (in relation to home finance activities, however the logic can be carried across in relation to other regulated activities) regarding the FSMA Test, that a degree of continuity is implied. As a result, one-off or extremely infrequent acts would usually not be thought to be enough to satisfy the test.

4.9.3.5 There is some helpful case law on this subject. One of the key cases is *Jackson v Ayles and another [2021] EWHC 995 (Ch)*. This case considered the enforceability of a loan under Section 26 of FSMA (during which the FSMA Test was considered). Here, it was found that the lending was carried out by way of business because:

(a) The relationship between the parties arose out of commercial dealings;

(b) The lending was "not built on trust";

(c) The lender had made a number of loans over the years to the borrowers and then separately to other individuals.

4.9.3.6 The case of *Bassano v Toft [2014] EWHC 377 QB* involved a person who dealt in musical instruments. When he made a loan which was secured against an instrument, this was not deemed to be carried on by way of business since his business was that of dealing in musical instruments and he did not ordinarily make loans as part of this business.

4.9.3.7 *Helden v Strathmore Ltd [2011] Bus LR 1592* involved the lender providing a number of informal loans to the borrower. This matter was considered by the Court of Appeal. One of the loans was for a large sum of money (£1 million) and this was secured against the borrower's home. Note that the lender sought to argue that the parties (the directors of the lender and the borrower) were friends, which meant that the lending could not be by way of business. It was concluded by the Court of Appeal that the lending was by way of business because of the number and regularity of loans, and the fact that they were for substantial sums of money. The loans were often documented formally and the connection between the lender (a limited company) and borrower was originally a professional one (the friendship developed out of this).

4.9.4 One is often asked to give a view on whether loans between family members are regulated. The high-level position is that these are unlikely to be regulated given the relationship of the parties is a family relationship and the lending is built on trust. Presumably, interest will not be charged and the lender does not regularly make loans. However, there are always exceptions to the general position and cases should be considered on their individual set of facts.

4.9.5 It is also worth considering the case of *Khodari v Al Tamimi [2008] EWHC 3065* which looked at lending between family members. Here the judge stated that "loans are explicable by the familial relationship", implying that generally lending between family members will not be regulated as it is unlikely that lending will ever be for business purposes but rather to help out a loved one.

4.9.6 Alteration of the business test for different regulated activities

4.9.6.1 The general starting point for investment business

(a) Article 3 of the Business Order amends the FSMA Test for these activities; for investment business, firms will not be carrying this on unless "they carry on the business of engaging in" activities that fall within Article 3 of the Business Order (the **Business Test**).

(b) These activities include:

(i) Dealing in investments as principal and agent;

(ii) Arranging deals in investments;

(iii) Operating an MTF or OTF;

(iv) Managing investments;

(v) Safeguarding and administering investments;

(vi) Sending dematerialised instructions;

(vii) Managing a UK UCITS or AIF;

(viii) Acting as a trustee or depositary of a UK UCITS or AIF;

(ix) Establishing a collective investment scheme;

(x) Advising on investments;

(xi) Agreeing to carry on any of the above, collectively known as investment business.

(c) In other words, if you are (for example) advising a person in relation to shares, the implication is that you will only do so if you "carry on the business of doing so" (in other words, you are in the business of providing investment advice rather than this being incidental to another type of business carried on by you). This is a much narrower test (as PERG tells us) as it means that the carrying on of the relevant regulated activity must represent the carrying on of a business in its own right.

(d) Therefore, for a person to be carrying on these activities they will usually need to do so with a degree of regularity and for commercial purposes (they will be expecting to gain a direct or indirect financial benefit of some kind and activities carried out because of friendship or for altruistic purposes will not normally be caught) (PERG 8.34.2 G).

(e) However the FCA clarifies:

(i) It is not necessary that a person seeks to profit from carrying on activities (the example given is a company providing investment research to other companies and charging to cover its costs); and

(ii) Services provided free of charge can amount to a business (for example advice may be free of charge but may be part of a business funded by fees or sponsorship).

(f) PERG 4.3.7 G confirms that an activity would need to be carried on with frequency and regularity to satisfy the Business Test.

(g) The difference between the FSMA Test and the Business Test is quite stark; a person would only be carrying on investment business if they carry on the business of doing so; this implies somewhat holding oneself out as providing the service. It is also essential that there is a degree of regularity and commerciality.

(h) I have had sight of counsel opinions which suggest that the service if carried on within a business must represent a separate workstream; one that is able to "stand on its own two feet" and could operate independently of the wider business to satisfy the Business Test.

(i) This can be contrasted with the FSMA Test, a person might by carrying on an activity by way of business even if they are not carrying on the business of doing so (for example, entering into regulated credit agreements as lender with some regularity).

(j) Factors that support the argument that a person is carrying on the business of engaging in investment business include: the frequency of the activity, the formality of the arrangements, a commercial element and whether or not the investment element is essential to the firm's main business activities.

4.9.7 Amendment of the FSMA Test for other regulated activities

4.9.7.1 The business element is altered for certain other regulated activities, for example accepting deposits (see Article 2(1) of the Business Order). This regulated activity will only be carried on if a person holds himself out as accepting deposits on a day-to-day basis (the FCA confirms that the more frequently these are accepted the less likely it is they would be deemed to be accepted only on particular occasions).

4.9.7.2 Similarly, a person who is carrying out insurance distribution will only do so if this is pursued for remuneration (which is defined as any commission, fee, charge or other payment, including an economic benefit of any kind or any other financial or non-financial advantage or incentive offered or given in respect of insurance distribution activities in the Insurance Distribution Directive (EU 2016/97). The FCA has confirmed at PERG 5.4.3 G that the concept of remuneration in the Business Order follows this definition.

4.9.7.3 Certain home finance activities will be carried on by way of business if provided on a one-off basis.

4.10 The link between regulated activities and the UK

4.10.1 The general prohibition confirms that a person will not be carrying on a regulated activity unless this is done in the UK (note that the UK does not include the Channel Islands or the Isle of Man).

4.10.2 While this concept sounds straightforward, depending on the circumstances, it may be difficult to establish if a regulated activity is being carried on from the UK (for example if the client is outside the UK or some other element of the activity happens outside the UK, as the FCA alludes to in PERG 2.4.1 G).

4.10.3 PERG has a section dedicated to the "link between activities and the United Kingdom" at PERG 2.4. There are also additional sections of PERG that relate to specific regulated activities which provide guidance on when the FCA considers that regulated activity to be carried on from the UK; these are disparate and scattered throughout the FCA Handbook. Some of these are gathered together below.

4.10.4 PERG 2.4 gives some indication of when the FCA considers that certain regulated activities are carried on from the UK. For example, a person situated in the UK and safeguarding and administering investments is deemed to be carrying on the activities in the UK even if the client is overseas (PERG 2.4.2 G).

4.10.5 PERG 2.4.3 G tells us that Section 418 of FSMA extends the meaning of "in the UK" by setting out additional cases. Section 418(4) FSMA mentions a UK based person where day-to-day management of the activity is the responsibility of an establishment in the UK.

4.10.6 A view can be taken that this is intended to demonstrate that a person does not need to have a registered or head office in the UK to carry on a regulated activity in the UK. This is confirmed at PERG 5.12.5 G in the context of insurance distribution activities where the FCA confirms that persons carrying on such activities from a registered or head office in the UK will "clearly" be carrying on regulated activities in the UK.

4.10.7 Further, Section 418(5) FSMA mentions the case of a person who is not based in the UK but is carrying on a regulated activity from an establishment in the UK.

4.10.8 PERG 2.4.3 G gives an example of a person managing investments where stages that make up the regulated activity take place in different countries. For example, management is in country A, assets are held by a nominee in country B, transactions take place in country C but all decisions about what to do with the investments are taken from an office in the UK.

4.10.9 PERG confirms in this scenario that even though investments are held and all dealings take place outside the UK, for the purposes of FSMA, the regulated activity of "managing investments" is carried on from the UK.

4.10.10 PERG 2.4.5 G talks about the activity of accepting deposits in the context of day-to-day management; this must not be the responsibility of a UK establishment.

4.10.11 For example, before FSMA, there were UK establishments that were representative offices of overseas institutions. PERG confirms that such institutions need to seek authorisation if the responsibility for the day-to-day management of the accepting of deposits by them outside the UK is effectively that of their UK establishment.

4.10.12 PERG 2.5.6 G references carrying on business in the UK even if there is no place of business maintained by that person in the UK (viz, via the internet or occasional visits). Here, the FCA tells us that a person should consider the Business Test (see above) and also the overseas persons exclusion (see part 6).

4.10.13 PERG 2.4.9 G tells us that if a credit agreement (or consumer hire agreement) is subject to the law of a country outside of the UK, a person can still be carrying out the regulated activity of credit broking in the UK (see PERG 2.7.7 E G).

4.10.14 PERG 5.12 provides guidance in relation to insurance related regulated activities but is very helpful for confirming the FCA's view on where the FCA considers regulated activities to be carried on.

4.10.15 PERG 5.12.6 G gives a suggested approach for determining the location of an activity, bearing in mind various factors including:

4.10.15.1 Section 418 of FSMA;

4.10.15.2 The nature of the activity; and

4.10.15.3 The overseas persons exclusion.

4.10.16 Where PERG 5.12.7 G does not apply, PERG 5.12.8 G tells us that we should consider further the nature of the activity in order to determine where it is carried on. I have always found this section of guidance very helpful for thinking conceptually about where a regulated activity is carried on. While this part of PERG relates to insurance, the logic can be applied across to other regulated activities:

4.10.16.1 Where arranging, this will usually be carried on in the location where the arranging takes place.

4.10.16.2 As for dealing, this will depend on many factors such as where the acceptance takes place, which will depend on the method of communication used.

4.10.16.3 As for advising, this is generally considered to take place where the advice is received.

4.10.17 The overseas persons exclusion is set out in the RAO at Article 72 (see part 6). PERG 5.12.9 G explains how this forms part of the link between regulated activities and the UK and confirms that it provides a potential exclusion for persons with no permanent place of business in the UK from which regulated activities are conducted or offers to conduct the regulated activities are made. There are two limbs to the overseas persons exclusion, which are examined in greater detail in section 6.

4.10.18 The case of *Financial Services Authority v Fradley and Woodward: [2004] EWHC 3008 (Ch)* provides some helpful insight into where the (then) Financial Services Authority (**FSA**) deemed regulated activities to be carried on. This case involved the operation of a collective investment scheme which involved collecting money from individuals and placing bets on horse races on their behalf. It was held that even though Mr Fradley had moved to Ireland the operation of the scheme was subject to FSMA. This was because the activities that took place in the UK were a significant part of the business activity of running the scheme (such as the maintenance of a bank account and a registered address for the business).

4.10.19 There are some observations to be made in relation to the link between regulated activities and the UK:

4.10.19.1 At times it can be complex to determine whether there is a sufficient UK nexus to deem a regulated activity to be carried on in the UK, all of the facts should be borne in mind to establish if there is enough of a UK nexus to bring the activities onshore in the UK;

4.10.19.2 Occasionally one is asked to consider what the impact is of providing a service via the internet, of course this may impact the UK nexus. If providing investment business via the internet (or offering) one must always consider the location of the recipient of the services and what this means from a regulatory perspective.

CHAPTER FIVE

THE SPECIFIED INVESTMENTS

5.1 PERG 2.5.1 G confirms to us that if the business element and link to the UK are satisfied one of the other key elements is that the relevant investments must be within the scope of the system of regulation.

5.2 The specified investments are listed at Part II of the RAO. In other words, a regulated activity cannot be carried out in the UK (by way of business) unless it relates to a specified investment as listed there.

5.3 There is significant guidance on the specified investments set out in PERG 2.6 and this guide examines some of the key specified investments in this section.

5.3.1 Deposits (Article 5(2) RAO)

5.3.1.1 PERG 2.6.2 G makes clear that a deposit is defined in article 5(2) of the RAO as follows:

(a) Deposit means a sum of money, (other than one excluded by any of articles 6 to 9A of the RAO) paid on terms:

(i) Under which it will be repaid, with or without

interest or premium, and either on demand or at a time or in circumstances agreed by or on behalf of the person making the payment and the person receiving it; and

(ii) Which are not referable to the provision of property (other than currency) or services or the giving of security.

5.3.1.2 Some of the wording in the definition is quite difficult to understand, but PERG helps us to comprehend that the definition of deposit focusses on a sum of money paid by one person to another on terms that it will be repaid when a specified event occurs (PERG 2.6.2 G).

5.3.1.3 PERG 2.6.3 G goes on to examine the exclusions from the activity of accepting deposits (referenced in the definition), including:

(a) Money paid in connection with certain transactions, such as advance payments for the provision of goods or services and sums paid to secure the performance of a contract (see Article 5(3) of the RAO).[1]

(b) Sums received in consideration for the issue of debt securities (Article 9 RAO).

(c) Sums received in exchange for electronic money (Article 9A). This guide does not cover the scope of the Electronic Money Regulations 2011 given that it is a more specialist regime, but I suggest considering PERG 3A for more on this topic.

5.3.1.4 PERG 2.6.4 G confirms that there are a set of different exclusions focussing on the identity of the person paying the money, or receiving it or both (for example, those

1 Article 5(3) confirms that the wording "money is paid on terms which are referable" as set out in part (b) of Article 5(2) if and only if it is paid by way of: advance or part payment under a contract for the sale, hire or other provision of property or services, and is repayable only in the event that the property or services is or are not in fact sold, hired or otherwise provided; security for the performance of a contract or by way of security in respect of loss which may result from the non-performance of a contract; or without prejudice to foregoing, security for delivery up or return of any property whether in a particular state of repair or otherwise.

that are linked in a specified way such as group companies or close relatives).

5.3.1.5 PERG 2.6.4-A G also examines structured deposits, which are a kind of deposit (PERG 2.6.4-A G). There are specific regulated activities that apply to structured deposits but not other types of deposit.

5.4 Electronic money (Article 74A RAO)

5.4.1 This guide will not cover electronic money noting that it forms part of a specialised regime, but it is important to note that e-money is specified as an investment in Article 74A of the RAO but only when issued by credit institutions, credit unions or municipal banks or persons deemed to have been granted authorisation under regulation 74 of the Electronic Money Regulations 2011 (or a person falling within regulation 76(1) of those regulations).

5.5 Rights under contracts of insurance (Article 3(1) RAO)

5.5.1 PERG confirms to us that there are two types of contracts of insurance:

5.5.1.1 General (Article 3(1), Part 1 of Schedule 1 of the RAO), which includes contracts of insurance such as accident, sickness, motor, aircraft, ships, damage to property, credit, legal expenses and financial loss, among others.

5.5.1.2 Long term (Article 3(1), Part II of Schedule 1 of the RAO), which includes life and annuity, permanent health etc. Note that policies that are the subject of a trust cannot be long-term insurance.

5.5.2 Further the RAO talks about a few other terms in relation to contracts of insurance, firstly qualifying contracts of insurance are known as life policies in the FCA Handbook. This means that they are long-term insurance contracts which are treated as contractually based investments.

5.5.3 The second term is relevant investments which applies to contractually based investments, encompassing life policies (but not rights to or interests in those rights) and rights under contracts of insurance other than life policies. This tends to link into regulated activities related to insurance distribution.

5.6 PERG 6 provides guidance to assist in deciding whether an arrangement is a contract of insurance.

5.7 PERG 6 confirms as follows:

5.7.1 The RAO, which sets out the activities for which authorisation is required, does not attempt an exhaustive definition of a 'contract of insurance'. Instead, it makes some specific extensions and limitations to the general common law meaning of the concept.

5.7.2 One consequence of this is that common law judicial decisions about whether particular contracts amount to 'insurance' or 'insurance business' are relevant in defining the scope of the FCA's authorisation and regulatory activities, as they were under predecessor legislation.

5.7.3 The courts have not fully defined the common law meaning of 'insurance' and 'insurance business', since they have, on the whole, confined their decisions to the facts before them. They have, however, given useful guidance in the form of descriptions of contracts of insurance.

5.7.4 The best established of these descriptions appears in the case *of Prudential v. Commissioners of Inland Revenue [1904] 2 KB 658*. This case, read with a number of later cases, treats as insurance any enforceable contract under which a 'provider' undertakes:

(1) in consideration of one or more payments;

(2) to pay money or provide a corresponding benefit (including in some cases services to be paid for by the provider) to a 'recipient';

(3) in response to a defined event the occurrence of which is uncertain (either as to when it will occur or as to whether it will occur at all) and adverse to the interests of the recipient.

5.7.5 The *Prudential* case is the starting point for the identification of a contract of insurance, any contracts that fall outside this description are unlikely to be contracts of insurance. The FCA will consider the principles set out in relation to the *Prudential* case in light of applicable legislation and case law.

5.7.6 The FCA will then apply the following principles of construction to determine if there is a contract of insurance:

(1) More weight attaches to the substance rather than the form of the contract; the form is not decisive of whether the contract is a contract of insurance: *Fuji Finance Inc. v. Aetna Life Insurance Co. Ltd [1997] Ch. 173 (C.A.).*

(2) The substance of the provider's obligation determines the substance of the contract: *re Sentinel Securities [1996] 1 WLR 316.* The FCA will not consider the provider or customer's intention or purpose relevant to its classification.

(3) The contract must be characterised as a whole and not according to its 'dominant purpose' or the relative weight of its 'insurance content': *Fuji Finance Inc. v. Aetna Life Insurance Co. Ltd [1997] Ch. 173 (C.A.).*

(4) A contract of insurance may be expressed in a number of documents.

5.7.7 Contracts under which the provider has an absolute discretion as to whether any benefit is provided on the occurrence of the uncertain event, are not contracts of insurance. This may be the case even if, in practice, the provider has never exercised its discretion so as to deny a benefit: *Medical Defence Union v. Department of Trade and Industry [1979] 2 W.L.R. 686.* My view is that PERG provides that discretion must always be exercised, it may just be that a claim is never denied.

5.7.8 The 'assumption of risk' by the provider is an important descriptive feature of all contracts of insurance.

5.7.9 Case law establishes that the provider's obligation under a contract of insurance is an enforceable obligation to respond (usually, by providing some benefit in the form of money or services) to the occurrence of the uncertain event. This guidance describes the assumption of that obligation as the 'assumption' by the provider of (all or part of) the insured risk. 'Transfer of risk' has the same meaning in this guidance.

5.7.10 Contracts, under which the amount and timing of the payments made by the recipient make it reasonable to conclude that there is a genuine pre-payment for services to be rendered in response to a future contingency, are unlikely to be regarded as insurance. In general, the FCA expects that this requirement will be satisfied where there is a commercially reasonable and objectively justifiable relationship between the amount of the payment and the cost of providing the contract benefit.

5.7.11 Contracts under which the provider undertakes to provide periodic maintenance of goods or facilities, whether or not any uncertain or adverse event (in the form of, for example, a breakdown or failure) has occurred, are unlikely to be contracts of insurance.

5.7.12 Under most commercial contracts with a customer, a provider will assume more than one obligation. Some of these may be insurance obligations, others may not. The FCA will consider the substance of the contract to determine whether there is a contract of insurance. If a provider provides an in substance insurance obligation then the FCA is likely to find that the provider has effected a contract of insurance (whether or not that obligation is substantial in comparison with the other contractual obligations).

5.7.13 A contract is more likely to be regarded as a contract of insurance if the amount payable by the recipient under the contract is calculated by reference to either or both of the probability of occurrence or likely severity of the uncertain event.

5.7.14 A contract is less likely to be regarded as a contract of insurance if it requires the provider to assume a speculative risk (ie a risk carrying the possibility of either profit or loss) rather than a pure risk (ie a risk of loss only).

5.7.15 A contract is more likely to be regarded as a contract of insurance if the contract…contains terms that are consistent with its classification as a contract of insurance, for example, obligations of the utmost good faith.

5.8 In *Re Digital Satellite Warranty Cover Limited* [2013] UKSC 7, the Supreme Court found that extended warranties for the repair and replacement of satellite television equipment were regulated insurance contracts for the purposes of the FSMA. Here, in consideration of a periodic payment satellite television dishes and associated equipment would be repaired or replaced in the event of breakdown, malfunction or physical damage. All three elements of the *Prudential* decision were present:

5.8.1 It was uncertain whether the equipment would break down in the period of cover.

5.8.2 The insured as owner has an insurable interest.

5.8.3 The provision of a repair and replacement service represents money or money's worth.

5.9 PERG 6.7 sets out some examples and discusses whether or not these are likely to be deemed to be contracts of insurance. One of the most interesting sections is around manufacturer and retailer warranties. Some firms looking to provide third party manufacturer warranties have attempted to take what are insurance contracts outside being regulated by describing these as service contracts for repair services, but the FCA has recently confirmed that they do not consider this to be an acceptable approach. These would have to be service contracts in the true sense for the repair of broken equipment for a fee; the service provider must not indemnify the customer against the uncertain cost of parts or replacement. There should be a relationship between the amount of payment and the cost of the benefit, with the provider standing ready to provide services on the occurrence of a future contingency.

5.10 **Shares etc (Article 76 RAO)**

5.10.1 PERG 2.6.9 G tells us that shares are defined in the RAO as shares or stock in many different types of entities, including any body corporate (wherever incorporated) and unincorporated bodies formed under the law of a country outside the UK.

5.10.2 The words "body corporate" are defined in relation to Section 417 of FSMA and capture all types of corporate bodies such as companies and partnerships of different types.

5.10.3 Shares in open-ended investment companies are excluded from being shares. Please see 5.12 below.

5.10.4 There are also exclusions for shares in the share capital of certain mutuals, which takes out of scope building society accounts. However, deferred shares issued by building societies will be caught since they are transferable and negotiable much like ordinary shares in a limited company.

5.10.5 Bearing in mind MiFID, the list of financial instruments in MiFID was onshored in Part 1 of Schedule 2 to the RAO (PERG 13.4). Transferable securities are defined in Article 4 and refer to classes of securities negotiable on the capital markets (capable of being traded on the capital markets).

5.11 Debt instruments (Article 77/78 RAO)

5.11.1 PERG 2.6.11 G rightly points out that the term "debt instruments" is divided into two categories: Private debt and public sector debt.

5.11.1.1 The first category is known as "instruments creating or acknowledging indebtedness" – Article 77 of the RAO. The FCA Handbook describes these as debentures, and this guide will refer to private debt as debentures for ease of reference. Article 77 covers debentures, bonds, loan stock and any other instrument creating or acknowledging indebtedness, which acts as a catchall in relation to private debt instruments.

5.11.1.2 The second category (Article 78) is linked to loan stock, bonds and other instruments creating or acknowledging indebtedness which are issued by or on behalf of any government (as well as assemblies for Scotland, Wales or Northern Ireland, a local authority or an international organisation).

5.11.2 PERG 2.6.11 G confirms that debt instruments (instrument meaning any record, this doesn't need to be in the form of a document) (Article 3(1) RAO) cannot be both categories – they need to be either Article 77 or Article 78 RAO.

5.11.3 This guide will not cover alternative finance bonds given that they are specialist instruments.

5.11.4 The case of *Levy v Abercorris Slate and Slab Co (1887) 37 Ch D 260* confirms that the term debenture is "not a term of art" but means simply any document that creates or acknowledges a debt.

5.11.5 Confusingly, from a financial services regulatory perspective, the Court of Appeal concluded in the case of *Fons Hf v (1) Corporal Ltd and another [2014] EWCA Civ 304* that a loan agreement is an instrument which creates and acknowledges a debt, and therefore a loan agreement could be a debenture and this a financial instrument. However, it is not an established market practice to treat banking market loans as debentures and as such specified investments.

5.12 Units (Article 81 RAO)

5.12.1 PERG 2.6.17 G confirms that this category refers to units in a collective investment scheme and covers units in a unit trust or authorised contractual scheme, shares in open-ended investment companies and rights in respect of most limited partnerships.

5.12.2 PERG rightly points out that shares in open-ended investment companies are different to shares in other companies; they are not treated as shares from a regulatory perspective but units in a collective investment scheme so this means that shares in open-ended investment companies are subject to restrictions on promotions of collective investment schemes (Section 238 of FSMA).

5.12.3 Exclusions related to collective investment schemes aren't set out in the RAO but in the CIS Order. Importantly, closed-ended bodies corporate are excluded from being collective investment schemes.

5.12.4 There is significant guidance on the meaning of open-ended investment company set out in PERG 9.

5.12.5 What is a CIS?

5.12.5.1 Section 235 (1) of the FSMA confirms that a "collective investment scheme" means any arrangements with respect to property of any description, including money, the purpose or effect of which is to enable persons taking part in the arrangements (whether by becoming owners of the property or any part of it or otherwise) to participate in or receive profits or income arising from the acquisition, holding, management or disposal of the property or sums paid out of such profit or income.

5.12.5.2 Section 235 (2) of the FSMA confirms that the arrangements must be such that the persons who are to participate do not have day-to-day control over the management of the property, whether or not they have the right to be consulted or to give directions.

5.12.5.3 Section 235 (3) of the FSMA confirms that the arrangements must have either or both of the following characteristics:

(a) the contributions of the participants and the profits or incomes out of which payments are to be made to them are pooled;

(b) the property is managed as a whole by or on behalf of the operator of the scheme.

5.12.5.4 There are exclusions that prevent certain arrangements from being a CIS, which appear in the schedule to the CIS Order (the **Schedule**).

5.12.5.5 Paragraph 4 of the Schedule confirms that arrangements do not amount to a CIS if they are operated otherwise than by way of business.

5.12.5.6 Paragraph 10 of the Schedule confirms that arrangements do not amount to a CIS if each of the participants is a body corporate in the same group as the operator.

5.12.5.7 Paragraph 21 of the Schedule confirms that no body corporate other than an open-ended investment company, amounts to a CIS. This does not apply to any body incorporated as a limited liability partnership. In other words, there is no specific carve-out for a partnership if it satisfies Section 235 FSMA.

5.12.5.8 Section 236 of FSMA confirms that an open-ended investment company means a CIS which satisfies both the property condition and the investment condition. There is significant detail on the meaning of these terms set out in PERG 9.

5.12.6 What is an AIF?

5.12.6.1 An AIF is an "alternative investment fund", a type of collective investment vehicle; when considering whether a CIS exists one typically must consider whether there is an AIF, as the two concepts are interlinked. The concept of an AIF was introduced through the European Alternative Investment Fund Managers Directive 2011 and is now enshrined and onshored into UK law.

5.12.6.2 PERG 16 contains very helpful guidance on what constitutes an AIF. This guide will not cover the AIF regime, but if you do need to consider whether an AIF exists, PERG 16 is the best place to start. It covers some of the key exemptions and carve-outs from the AIF regime, such as joint ventures and family investment vehicles.

5.12.6.3 To raise some high-level points around the definition of an AIF, PERG highlights that the FCA's approach to deciding whether something is an AIF is as follows (Question 1.4):

(a) When defining what an AIF is, the drafters of AIFMD faced a dilemma. If there is a precise and detailed definition there is a risk that some funds that should be regulated would fall outside regulation, given the wide variety of legal forms they can take. However, a broad definition entails a risk that AIFMD is given a much wider scope than intended. The agreed definition of AIF is drafted at a high level of generality and uses words which have a wide meaning.

5.12.6.4 The basic definition of an AIF is as follows (Question 2.1):

(a) For the purposes of the AIFMD regime in the United Kingdom, an AIF is a collective investment undertaking, including investment compartments of such an undertaking, which:

(i) raises capital from a number of investors, with a view to investing it in accordance with a defined investment policy for the benefit of those investors; and

(ii) is not a UK UCITS.

(b) The key elements of the definition are:

(i) it is a collective investment undertaking (CIU);

(ii) it has a defined investment policy;

(iii) it raises capital with a view to investing that capital for the benefit of those investors in accordance with that policy;

(iv) an AIF does not include a UK UCITS.

(c) It is necessary to satisfy all the elements of the definition in order to be an AIF.

5.13 Options (Article 83 RAO)

5.13.1 At a high level, an option gives the person who acquires it the right to acquire or dispose of certain financial instruments, currencies or commodities at a certain price and at a future date.

5.13.2 PERG 2.6.20 G confirms that this category includes:

5.13.2.1 Options to acquire or dispose of securities or contractually based investments, currency and certain precious metals and options to acquire or dispose of such options.

5.13.2.2 Note that options to buy or sell other types of commodity only fall within this category if they are:

(a) options to buy or sell futures or options to buy or sell CFDs. Other options to buy or sell other types of commodity may be CFDs.

(b) Options to acquire or dispose of other property which must fall within certain paragraphs of Schedule 2 of the RAO to be options.

(c) Options to acquire or dispose of those falling within (b), but only when PERG 2.5.7 G applies.

5.13.2.3 PERG confirms that options that aren't listed at (a) above (PERG gives the example of physically settled options on non-precious metals) must meet the conditions in (b) to be options.

5.13.2.4 PERG 2.6.20A confusingly mentions that if an option is only an option because of part (b), it will be an option only in relation to the services referred to in PERG 2.5.8 G provided by that person (and the same goes if they are part (c) options), such as an option on a physically settled copper option traded on a regulated market (as explained in PERG).

5.13.2.5 In relation to considering the position on derivatives, it is not enough to consider the position as to the RAO, it is very important to consider the PERG guidance relating to MiFID to have a full picture.

5.14 Futures (Article 84 RAO)

5.14.1 PERG confirms that futures are rights under a contract for the sale of a commodity or property of any other description, under which delivery is to be made at a future date and at a price agreed on when the contract is made (PERG 2.6.21 G).

5.14.2 PERG 2.6.22 G, states that the key issue in determining whether something is an investment in this category for the purposes of the RAO is whether the contract is made for investment rather than commercial purposes.

5.14.3 Contracts made for commercial purposes are excluded and the RAO sets out a number of tests as to when an investment in this category is commercial rather than being for investment purposes.

5.14.4 PERG also explains that there are an additional category of instruments which are futures in only limited circumstances. This is because they fail one of the above-mentioned tests, and satisfy certain other criteria as set out in Article 84(1A)-(1D) of the RAO.

5.15 Contracts for differences etc (Article 85 RAO)

5.15.1 The final category of derivatives is set out at PERG 2.6.23 G where it is confirmed that this category covers:

5.15.1.1 Rights under contracts for differences (**CFDs**) (which is very unhelpful!). If you follow through to the definition for CFDs, this is linked to the definition set out in the RAO which again references CFDs, which is of course circular. It is quite common to come across these issues when looking at the regulatory framework. In summary, CFDs are contracts where a person agrees to pay the other the difference between the opening and closing price of an asset without owning the asset itself.

5.15.1.2 Rights under other contracts whose purpose (or pretended purpose) is to secure a profit or avoid by loss of reference to fluctuations in certain factors (PERG tells us this includes the value or price of property of any description or an index, or any factor designated in the contract) and derivative contracts for the transfer of credit risk (not set out above) within paras 8 or 9 of Part 1 of Schedule 2 to the RAO, but only when PERG 2.5.7 G applies, will also be CFDs.

5.15.2 It is important to note that CFDs are always cash-settled instruments (PERG 2.6.23A G).

5.15.3 Certain contracts that might fall within this category (PERG mentions spread bets and interest rate swaps) may well have been treated as gaming contracts (and as a result be unenforceable) but for the existence of Section 412 of FSMA (gaming contracts) (PERG 2.6.23A G).

5.15.4 PERG 2.6.24 G notes that an exclusion applies if the parties intend that the profit is to be secured or the loss to be avoided by taking delivery of property.

5.15.5 Binary and fixed options bets can also be treated as CFDs (PERG 2.6.24A G covers this). A product will be binary only if the payout is all or nothing; the overall result is that one party pays the other a fixed sum, for example a binary or digital option (see PERG 2.6.24A G (2)). A fixed option bet has a number of possible payouts and they are all known in advance, however it differs from a binary contract because the number of possible payouts is more than just two (three or more) PERG 2.6.24A G (6).

5.15.6 Interestingly, a simple binary sporting bet is not a CFD because it is not covered by MiFID (PERG 2.6.24A (1) (d) G tells us a binary bet can only be a CFD if it is a financial instrument falling within paras 4 to 7 or 10 of part 1 of Schedule 2 to the RAO) and it does not come under any other part of the definition of a CFD (PERG 2.6.24A (5) G).

5.16 Additional categories of investments

5.16.1 Lloyd's investments and rights to or interests in certain contracts or investments (will not be dealt with under this section. However, it is worth noting that rights to or interests in all specified investments are themselves treated as specified investments.

5.16.2 Rights under regulated mortgage contracts and regulated credit agreements are also specified investments. Again, as specialist regimes these will not be covered under this general guide.

CHAPTER SIX

THE REGULATED ACTIVITIES AND THE EXCLUSIONS

6.1 PERG 2.5.1 G refers to a second element which is essential for a regulated activity to be deemed to be carried on in the UK, specifically that in relation to the specified investments that this guide has examined at part 5, that the activities in relation to those specified investments are actually regulated under FSMA.

6.2 You will find the "regulated activities" set out in the RAO. PERG 2.7 considers each of these in detail.

6.3 **How exclusions are dealt with in this guide**

6.3.1 There are two sets of exclusions to be aware of:

6.3.1.1 **Specific Exclusions:** those that relate to particular regulated activities and the application of which relates to the specifics of that regulated activity; and

6.3.1.2 **General Exclusions:** those that are more general and provide exclusions in relation to a set of different regulated activities.

6.3.2 Note that a person will not require authorisation pursuant to FSMA if an activity is excluded pursuant to the RAO.

6.3.3 The way in which applicable exclusions are dealt with in relation the regulated activities listed below is as follows:

6.3.3.1 Where a Specific Exclusion applies to a regulated activity, the subject matter of that exclusion will be dealt with under the paragraph dealing with that regulated activity.

6.3.3.2 General Exclusions will be dealt in detail at 6.16 and their availability will be listed out under each regulated activity.

6.3.3.3 Where an exclusion is modified or not available for a MiFID investment firm, an asterix will be placed next to that exclusion.

6.3.4 The exclusions set out below are the "key" exclusions, although they represent a non-exhaustive list of those which are available. Note as well there are exclusions for entities such as local authorities, which this guide has not covered as it is not intended for Government bodies.

6.4 Overrides

6.4.1 When looking at the exclusions to the regulated activities set out in the RAO, it is crucial to consider if any "overrides" apply. Overrides can loosely be described as the way in which European legislation was laid on top of the existing UK framework. The way that the overrides have been imposed can seem quite clumsy, and one must be aware of their existence as sometimes it is not obvious that they apply.

6.4.2 PERG 2.5.3 G explains that the application of certain exclusions is modified in relation to persons who are subject to the UK provisions that implemented MiFID, the Insurance Distribution Directive and the Mortgage Credit Directive. As this guide considers the general regimes relating to investment activities it will only examine the MiFID override for the purposes of this section.

6.5 The concept of a MiFID investment firm

6.5.1 Persons subject to the UK provisions implementing MiFID had to be brought in scope under the FSMA (PERG 2.5.4 G).

6.5.2 This section of PERG explains that a core element of MiFID is the concept of a MiFID "investment firm": any person whose regular occupation or business is the provision of one or more MiFID investment services to third parties, or the performance of these on a professional basis.

6.5.3 I have found that it can be difficult to understand what is meant by MIFID investment firm, but one might take the view that this is an entity that provides or performs MiFID investment services professionally.

6.5.4 For example, an entity that provides investment advice on an ongoing basis for a fee and holds itself out as providing such advice might be a MiFID investment firm.

6.6 Exemptions from MiFID

6.6.1 An investment firm will not be subject to the UK provisions which implemented MiFID if it falls within one or more of the exemptions set out in Part 1 Schedule 3 of the RAO. Further information on these is set out in PERG 13.5.

6.6.2 Note however if a firm is not a MiFID investment firm because an exemption in Part 1, Schedule 3 of the RAO applies, it may still be carrying on UK regulated activities and therefore require authorisation.

6.7 The MiFID Override

6.7.1 PERG 2.5.5 G explains that some of the exclusions in the RAO (applying to persons who are not caught by MiFID) are made unavailable to MIFID investment firms when they provide or perform MiFID investment services.

6.7.2 The important section of the RAO is Article 4(4) which lists a number of exclusions that must be disregarded including the exclusion for groups and joint enterprises.

6.7.3 Briefly examining the group exclusion, the definition of group pursuant to MiFID is narrower than that under the RAO, so if you are looking to benefit from the group exclusion for a firm carrying on MiFID investment services, it is the narrower MiFID test of group that should be borne in mind.

6.7.4 PERG 13.5 at Question 37 confirms that the MiFID version of the group exclusion confirms that you can provide certain MiFID services to your parent company, subsidiaries and the subsidiaries of your parent company. As mentioned above, PERG highlights that the MiFID exemption is narrower than the corresponding exclusion in Article 69 of the RAO because it does not apply to investment services supplied to a joint venture participant (which is allowed pursuant to Article 69 RAO through the use of the term "participating interest").

6.7.5 This guide will not examine how MiFID amends each regulated activity, but flags where it is important to consider the override in relation to the relevant exclusion.

6.8 What is an exempt person?

6.8.1 PERG 2.10.1 G deals with exempt persons. This section of PERG explains that there are various provisions that disapply the General Prohibition from specific persons in relation to the carrying on by them of particular regulated activities.

6.8.2 Section 417(1) of FSMA confirms that the following are exempt persons:

6.8.2.1 Those that are exempt from the general prohibition in respect of an activity as a result of the FSMA (Exemption) Order 2001, for example the Bank of England is exempt from the general prohibition despite carrying on activities that may be deemed to be regulated activities;

6.8.2.2 Appointed representatives under Section 39 of FSMA: or

6.8.2.3 Recognised investment exchanges (for example, the London Stock Exchange) or recognised clearing houses.

6.8.3 At a high level an appointed representative is a person that has been "appointed" by a regulated principal firm to carry out certain regulated activities (as set out in the agreement between the two entities) underneath the principal's regulatory umbrella. This allows the appointed representative to carry on certain regulated activities without being directly authorised by the FCA. Appointed representatives do appear on the Financial Services Register.

THE REGULATED ACTIVITIES

6.9 Accepting Deposits (Article 5 RAO)

6.9.1 PERG 2.7.2 G confirms to us that whether or not the activity of accepting deposits is a regulated activity depends on the use to which the money is put.

6.9.2 If money received by way of deposit is *lent to others* or if any other activity of the person accepting the deposit is financed wholly (or to a material extent) out of the capital of, or interest on money received by way of deposit, the activity will constitute the regulated activity of accepting deposits.

6.9.3 PERG confirms that generally accepting deposits is the only regulated activity that applies to the specified investment deposits, however structured deposits have their own separate regime where there are certain regulated activities applying to structured deposits such as dealing as agent, arranging (bringing about) deals in investments etc.

6.9.4 **General Exclusions**

6.9.4.1 There are only two available General Exclusions to this activity, as set out at PERG 2.8.2 G.

6.9.4.2 The first relates to firms with permission to manage an AIF or a UK UCITS and means activities carried on by them in connection with the purposes of this management activity are excluded from being regulated activities.

6.9.4.3 Further activities carried on by local authorities are excluded from the activity of accepting deposits.

6.10 Dealing in investments (as principal or agent) (Articles 14 and 21 RAO)

6.10.1 PERG 2.7.6 G confirms that the activities of dealing in investments as principal and dealing in investments as agent are defined in terms of buying, selling, subscribing for or underwriting certain investments which are:

6.10.1.1 for dealing as principal: Securities or Contractually based investments; and

6.10.1.2 for dealing as agent: Securities, structured deposits and relevant investments.

6.10.2 PEG 2.7.6A G notes that "buying" is defined in the RAO as including acquiring for valuable consideration. "Selling" is defined to include disposing for valuable consideration (disposing itself is defined so that it covers a range of possible transactions according to the nature of the investment being transferred).

6.10.3 Importantly, dealing as principal in relation to Securities (or life policies) is a regulated activity <u>only</u> if the exclusion in Article 15 of the RAO does not apply (Absence of holding out etc).*

6.10.4 PERG 2.8.4 G (1) tells us that the Article 15 exclusion superimposes an *additional condition* that needs to be met before a person "dealing as principal" is deemed to be carrying on a regulated activity.

6.10.5 The person must therefore "hold himself out" as "making a market" in the relevant specified investments, or as being in the business in dealing in them, or he must regularly solicit members of the public without the purposes of inducing them to deal. This is the key test for dealing as principal; you can't do the regulated activity unless you hold yourself out.

6.10.6 The Specific Exclusions for dealing as principal

6.10.7 While the above-mentioned "exclusion" in Article 15 should always be borne in mind to establish whether a person is dealing in investments as principal (in other words, the person must hold themselves out as dealing as principal), there are a number of other available exclusions in relation to this regulated activity which are listed out at PERG 2.8.4 G.

6.10.8 PERG 2.8.4 (2) (G) confirms that entering into a transaction relating to a Contractually based investment will not be regulated if it is entered into by an unauthorised person in the following circumstances:

6.10.8.1 Where the person with whom they deal with is either authorised or exempt for the relevant business; or

6.10.8.2 Where the person enters into a transaction through a non-UK office (PERG provides this could actually be his own) and he deals with or through someone who is based outside the UK who as his ordinary business carries on regulated activities.*

6.10.9 Further, a person providing someone else with finance can accept an instrument acknowledging the debt without dealing as principal (PERG 2.8.4 (3) G).

6.10.10 It is also helpful that PERG has confirmed that a company does not deal as principal if it is issuing its own shares or share warrants, and a person does not deal as principal by issuing his own debentures, alternative debentures, debenture warrants or alternative debenture warrants (PERG 2.8.4 (4) G).

6.10.11 General Exclusions for dealing as principal

6.10.11.1 The general exemptions that apply to this activity are (the asterix means that MiFID investment firms can't use them):

(a) Acting as bare trustee;

(b) Sale of goods or services*;

(c) Group exclusion* (can be used by MIFID firm, but must use the MiFID definition of group);

(d) Sale of body corporate*;

(e) Employee share scheme; and

(f) Overseas person.

6.10.12 Specific Exclusions for dealing as agent

6.10.12.1 There is an exclusion for transactions entered into by an agent who is not authorised but deals with someone who is an authorised person (see Article 22 RAO). The agent must not give any advice and he must not receive any remuneration unless account is made to the client. *

6.10.13 General Exclusions for dealing as agent

6.10.13.1 Further a number of the General Exclusions apply to a person dealing as agent:

(a) In connection with carrying on a profession or business not otherwise consisting of regulated activities; *

(b) In connection with the sale of goods or services; *

(c) The group exclusion;*

(d) In connection with the sale of a body corporate; *

(e) In connection with an employee share scheme;

(f) As an overseas person;

(g) On behalf of participants of a business angel-led enterprise capital fund; *

(h) In connection with managing a UK UCITS or AIF;

(i) When acting as insolvency practitioner.

6.11 Arranging deals in investments (Article 25 RAO)

6.11.1 There are two key activities to be aware of that are set out at Article 25 of the RAO:

6.11.1.1 Article 25 (1) of the RAO is the regulated activity of arranging (bringing about) deals in investments.

6.11.1.2 Article 25(2) of the RAO is the regulated activity of making arrangements with a view to transactions in investments.

6.11.2 There is significant guidance on the arranging regulated activities set out both in PERG 2 but also in the sections that relate to insurance distribution (PERG 5), that can be borne in mind when considering investment services.

6.11.3 The activity of "arranging (bringing about)" (Article 25(1)) is intended to catch arrangements that have the *direct effect* that a particular transaction is concluded (in other words, the arrangements directly bring it about) (PERG 2.7.7B G).

6.11.4 The "making arrangements" (Article 25(2)) activity is much wider (and acts as something of a catch-all). It is this activity that can be particularly difficult to avoid carrying on since it is so broadly drafted (and in fact the insurance distribution guidance casts a particularly wide net). PERG confirms that this activity is concerned with arrangements of an ongoing nature whose purpose is to facilitate the entering into of transactions by other parties (PERG 2.7.7B G).

6.11.5 PERG sets out two scenarios where it is likely that the making arrangements activity is likely to be carried on. The first is to enable or assist investors to deal with or through a particular firm (note that PERG specifically references the arrangements made by introducers here, which implies that the FCA envisages that mere introducing can constitute the regulated activity of making arrangements.

6.11.6 The second is to facilitate the entering into of transactions directly by parties (such as multilateral trading facilities of any kind (other than those excluded under Article 25(3) of the RAO) and other large organisations like exchanges and clearing houses) (PERG 2.7.7B G).

6.11.7 Further, the making arrangements activity is not limited to arrangements participated in by investors; PERG gives the example of a company making arrangements with a view to their issuing of investments (PERG 2.7.7BA G).

6.11.8 Helpfully, the FCA confirms their view that generally it will be the case that providers of back-office admin facilities are not making arrangements (because they aim to assist a broker firm to deal with the aftermath of transactions it has entered into on behalf of clients). When it outsources functions, the back office of the broker firm is making arrangements to assist the broker to enter into trades as agent for its clients; the transaction has already been entered into before back office involvement (PERG 2.7.7BC G).

6.11.9 The High Court examined the scope of Article 25(2) RAO in relation to the concept of introducing in *Watersheds Limited v. David Da Costa and Paul Gentlemen.*

6.11.10 Here it was decided that the activity of introducing in of itself doesn't constitute Article 25(2) "making arrangements". This is somewhat at odds to the views of the FCA that imply that introducing can in fact constitute article 25(2) "making arrangements". The FCA has confirmed that the judgment should be considered "in the light of the case to which it relates." I have taken this to mean that the FCA considers that the case was specific to its facts, and that introducing can (in the eyes of the FCA) fall within scope of the "making arrangements" activity.

6.11.11 The FCA states at PERG 2.7.7BD G that the court does not seem to have had the benefit of a relevant argument in the sense that the RAO has an exclusion in relation to introductions (Article 33 RAO) when it comes to Article 25(2) RAO.

6.11.12 The FCA makes the point that the exclusion would not exist if all introductions were outside the scope of the making arrangements activity. As a result, the FCA's view is that certain arrangements for making introductions can come within the scope of the Article 25(2) activity, however the FCA recognises that the judgment in Watersheds "introduces an element of doubt".

6.11.13 Some of the most helpful guidance on the boundaries of the Article 25(2) activity is found at PERG 2.7.7

BF G; it is this guidance that I return to regularly when writing legal opinions. This guidance confirms that a mere passive display of literature advertising investments will not amount to the article 25(2) activity. PERG 5.6.4 G (which relates to insurance distribution but examines the same concept) provides that leaving leaflets advertising a product in a waiting room and doing no more would not amount to the article 25(2) activity. This implies that "doing more" than something passive (leaving out product literature for someone to pick up) will amount to article 25(2).

6.11.14 PERG 5.6.4 G is also very helpful when considering the boundaries of Article 25(2). While the guidance is related to insurance distribution, the FCA confirms that the principles set out here are not limited to such activities. This section talks about Article 25(2) catching the activities of people who help fill in or check applications *in the context of ongoing arrangements* between the customer and (here) insurance undertakings. A further example given is a person introducing customers to an intermediary, for advice or to help arrange (whether an oral or written introduction).

6.11.15 Clients regularly ask for advice on the boundaries of Article 25(2) as there are many persons who wish to introduce potential investors in relation to a fundraising for a fee. Unfortunately Article 25(2) is very broadly drafted which means that there is not much that can be done in this regard without carrying on a regulated activity. There is further guidance in PERG 5 which suggests that passing on client contact details to a broker on an on-going basis will be enough to be caught under Article 25(2), which implies that very little can be done without being caught by the activity.

6.11.16 What this suggests is that it is acceptable to pass on client contact details once, however a contract that provides for referrals and introductions to be made on an ongoing basis is likely to trigger the Article 25(2) activity.

6.11.17 There is some helpful guidance on the arranging activities in PERG 8.32 which tells us that Article 25(1) only applies where the arrangements bring about or would bring about the particular transaction in question (because of the exclusion in Article 26 RAO) (see reference to Article 26 below). The FCA tells us that a person will only bring about or would bring about a transaction if *his involvement in the chain of events leading to the transaction is of enough importance that without that involvement it would not take place* (PERG 8.32.2 G). This is in contrast to article 25(2) which is much wider as it does not require that the arrangements actually bring about particular transactions.

6.11.18 **Specific Exclusions for arranging**

6.11.18.1 The exclusions relating to arranging are available depending on the type of arranging carried on, whether it is Article 25(1) or Article 25(2) arranging.

6.11.18.2 PERG 2.8.6A (1) examines article 26 RAO, which provides that arrangements that do not or would not bring about the transaction to which they relate are excluded from arranging activities that relate to a particular transaction only. A person will "bring about" a transaction only if their involvement in the chain of events leading to a transaction is of sufficient importance that, without that involvement, it would not take place.

6.11.18.3 Under Article 27 RAO, providing the means by which parties to a transaction (or possible transaction) are able to communicate with each other is excluded from arrangements made with a view to persons entering in certain transactions (PERG 2.8.6A G (2)). This exclusion is made available for persons such as internet service providers where they only provide communication facilities (and this might constitute arrangements made with a view).

6.11.18.4 If the arranger is a party to a transaction, this is excluded from Article 25(1) and Article 25(2) pursuant to Article 28 RAO (PERG 2.8.6A (3) G). This exclusion ensures a person is not regarded as arranging deals for someone else if the transaction is one where he intends to be a party. There are some carve outs if the transaction involves a contract of insurance.

6.11.18.5 Article 29 RAO confirms that someone who acts on behalf of a client to arrange transactions with or through an authorised person is excluded from arranging activities (although there are some requirements around not providing advice and disclosing remuneration) (PERG 2.8.6A (4) G).*

6.11.18.6 There are some exclusions for the making of arrangements for the entering into of finance under Articles 31 and 32.

6.11.18.7 This guide has already touched on Article 33 (introducing) when considering the scope of Article 25.

6.11.18.8 Article 34 confirms that a company is not carrying on a regulated activity by arranging for the issue of its shares or share warrants.*

6.11.19 General Exclusions

6.11.19.1 The following General Exclusions apply to the arranging activities:

(a) Acting as trustee;

(b) Carrying on a profession or business;*

(c) Sale of goods or services;*

(d) Group exclusion;*

(e) Sale of body corporate;*

(f) Employee share schemes;

(g) Overseas persons.

6.12 Managing investments (Article 37 RAO)

6.12.1 PERG 2.7.8 G confirms that the regulated activity involves the following elements:

6.12.1.1 The exercise of discretion, which must be exercised in relation to the composition of the portfolio under management.

6.12.1.2 That the property belongs beneficially to another person (this means that if a person manages his own property he is not carrying on the regulated activity). Note that if you are acting as trustee and managing the assets of a trust this may be caught.

6.12.1.3 The property to be managed consists of (or includes) Securities, structured deposits or Contractually based investments (or it is possible it could consist of or include these, for example there has been a representation that there would be such an investment).

6.12.2 General Exclusions

6.12.2.1 The following General Exclusions apply:

(a) Acting as trustee;

(b) Sale of goods or supply of services;*

(c) Group exclusion.*

6.12.3 It is worth mentioning that this guide does not cover the "collective portfolio management" activities. Collective portfolio management refers to fund management type activities, including the following:

6.12.3.1 Managing a UK UCITS;

6.12.3.2 Acting as trustee or depositary of a UK UCITS;

6.12.3.3 Managing an AIF;

6.12.3.4 Acting as trustee or depositary of an AIF; and

6.12.3.5 Establishing, operating and winding up a collective investment scheme.

6.12.4 It is helpful to think of these activities as referring to a collective type of management activity (for example, where persons assets are managed collectively under one overarching investment strategy) whereas the managing investments activity normally relates to management carried on in relation to a single mandate or a single investor.

6.13 Safeguarding and administering investments (Article 40 RAO)

6.13.1 PERG 2.7.9 G confirms that if a person safeguards and administers investments (which are securities or contractually based investments) which belong to another person, this is regulated. So is undertaking to arrange on a continuing basis for others to carry out the safeguarding and administering. These are generally to be regarded as the services carried on by a custodian.

6.13.2 Note that both safeguarding and administering activities must be present before a person will be carrying on a regulated activity.

6.13.3 PERG describes safeguarding as acting as custodian of the property (an example is given of holding documents that evidence the investments). Administration is the provision of services to the owner (or manager) of the property (such as settling sale transactions, dealing with income, dealing with corporate actions).

6.13.4 PERG makes the point that normally admin services will not allow the custodian discretion.

6.13.5 **Specific Exclusions**

6.13.5.1 PERG 2.8.8 G comments on the exclusions for this activity and confirms at (1) that these activities carried on by one person are excluded if a specified third party undertakes a responsibility for the assets which is no less onerous than it would have been if he were doing the safeguarding and administration himself. PERG tells us what this means in practice is that an authorised person who has permission to do this activity can delegate the activities without the delegate needing to be authorised and without loss of protection to the owner of the assets.

6.13.5.2 It is also excluded to introduce to an authorised or exempt person (see PERG 2.7.9 G), PERG 2.8.8 (2) G.

6.13.5.3 There are certain activities (PERG tells us) that are excluded from even being part of the activity of administration; a person won't be carrying on a regulated activity if these are the only activities carried on. The reason for this PERG explains at part (3) is because a person must be carrying on both the activity of safeguarding and that of administration, or arranging for both to be carried on by someone else to be carrying on the actual regulated activity.

6.13.6 General Exclusions

6.13.6.1 The following general exclusions apply:

(a) Acting as trustee;

(b) Carrying on of a business;

(c) Sale of goods or services;

(d) Group exclusion;

(e) Employee share schemes.

6.14 Advising on investments (Article 53 RAO)

6.14.1 Providing guidance on the scope of the advising on investments activity is one of my preferred tasks because the guidance on this regulated activity is very detailed and helpfully set out in PERG. There is significant guidance on the regulated activity of advising on investments, in fact there are entire sections of PERG dedicated to the nuances of this particular regulated activity.

6.14.2 The most helpful guidance on the regulated activity of advising on investments is set out in PERG 8.24.

6.14.3 Note that the guidance set out in this section does not constitute a specific exclusion to this regulated activity but merely advice on scope; considering this guidance is ordinarily the easiest way to get comfortable as to whether or not advising a client constitutes regulated investment advice.

6.14.4 This section begins by confirming that advising on investments is advice which:

6.14.4.1 Is given to a person in his capacity as an investor or potential investor, or in his capacity as agent for an investor or a potential investor; and

6.14.4.2 Is advice on the merits of his (whether as principal or agent):

(a) Buying, selling, subscribing for, exchanging, redeeming, holding or underwriting a particular investment which is a Security, a structured deposit or relevant investment; or

(b) Exercising or not exercising any right conferred by such an investment to buy, sell, subscribe for, exchange or redeem such an investment.

6.14.5 Note that if a person is authorised to provide regulated activities other than advising on investments, that person will only be advising on investments if they are providing a personal recommendation (PERG 8.24.1A G).

6.14.6 A firm that is not otherwise authorised will need permission for advising on investments. But if a firm is otherwise authorised, it can give non-personalised advice (viz investment advice that is not a personal recommendation) without the need to have advising on investments in its permission; it will be an unregulated activity for the firm. If it wishes to provide personal recommendations then its permission must include advising on investments (PERG 8.24.1B G).

6.14.7 PERG 8.30B goes into detail on the meaning of a personal recommendation. This a recommendation that:

6.14.7.1 Is made to a person in their capacity as an investor or potential investor or agent for an investor or a potential investor;

6.14.7.2 Is for the person to advise on investments (as defined above);

6.14.7.3 Is presented as suitable for the person to whom it is made or based on a consideration of the circumstances of that person; and

6.14.7.4 Is not issued exclusively to the public.

6.14.8 Of course, the definition of personal recommendation in the RAO derives from the MiFID investment service, which means it needs to be interpreted in line with MiFID (PERG 8.30B.3 G). However, the types of investments to which the recommendation relates are not limited to ones covered in MiFID, PERG confirms.

6.14.9 PERG 8.25.1 G confirms that advising on investments must relate to securities or relevant investments.

6.14.10 PERG 8.26 confirms that advice must relate to a particular investment and generic or general advice will not be investment advice (it may however be a Financial Promotion). The examples of generic advice include:

6.14.10.1 Financial planning;

6.14.10.2 Advice on the merits of investing in Japan rather than in Europe;

6.14.10.3 Advice on the merits of investing in investment trusts as opposed to unit trusts or unit-linked insurance.

6.14.11 PERG 8.27 confirms that advice must be given to persons in their capacity as investors (on the merits of their investing as principal or agent).

6.14.12 Note that a person will not be providing investment advice where the advice is given to an adviser who may use it to inform advice given by him to other persons (where he does not act as agent) (PERG 8.27.2 G), or if he does act as agent and it doesn't relate to the transaction into which the person is to enter as agent (PERG 8.27.3 G).

6.14.13 To the contrary, there will be investment advice where the recipient is someone who invests on behalf of other persons such as a trustee or nominee or discretionary fund manager where he receives the advice in that capacity (PERG 8.27.4 G).

6.14.14 One of the most helpful parts of the PERG 8 guidance on investment advice is that set out at PERG 8.28 which provides guidance on what the FCA considers to be "mere" information and what it considers to be regulated investment advice.

6.14.15 PERG 8.28.1 G confirms that in the FCA's view, advice needs an element of opinion on the part of the adviser; it is a recommendation as to action to take.

Information however, in contrast, involves statements of fact or figures.

6.14.16 The FCA further confirms that giving information without making any comment or value judgement is not investment advice (PERG 8.28.2 (1) G); it is a question of whether the communication goes beyond the mere provision of information and is objectively likely to influence the customer's decision whether or not to buy or sell (PERG 8.28.2 (3) G).

6.14.17 The FCA gives some further examples of what may generally constitute information (as opposed to investment advice), including:

6.14.17.1 Listings of share and unit prices;

6.14.17.2 Company news / announcements;

6.14.17.3 An explanation of the terms and conditions of an investment;

6.14.17.4 A comparison of the benefits and risks of one investment as compared to another;

6.14.17.5 Alerting persons to the happening of certain events (for example, should a particular share reach a certain price),

in other words, providing clients with this type of information will not constitute the provision of regulated advice.

6.14.18 Note however that the FCA makes the point that information could indeed become advice depending on the circumstances in which it is provided where this turns it into a recommendation (the issue of alerting a person to shares achieving a certain value depends on context, perhaps they have offered to do so when they think it is a good time to sell them) (PERG 8.28.4 G).

6.14.19 PERG 8.29.1 G further confirms that advice must relate to the buying, holding or selling of an investment, the FCA describes this as the pros and cons of doing so.

6.14.20 Sometimes financial planning firms do not have permission to give investment advice because their advice does not constitute regulated advice because it is generic and high level. Linked into this is PERG 8.29.2 G, which tells us that an explanation of the implications of exercising certain rights or happening of certain events (the example given is what happens on death) does not implicitly involve advice on the merits of exercising those rights.

6.14.21 It is also confirmed that it is acceptable to provide advice on the advantages of using a particular stockbroker or investment manager because this is also not advice on the merits of buying or selling an investment (PERG 8.29.3 G).

6.14.22 PERG 8.29.5 G gives some specific examples of the types of services that are not likely to be investment advice:

6.14.22.1 Interpreting the likely meaning of certain (uncertain) provisions in an investment agreement (which is fortunate, as it would otherwise mean that the activities of lawyers are caught (although arguably, there are other exclusions that may be helpful in relation to the activities of lawyers));

6.14.22.2 How to complete an application for an investment;

6.14.22.3 The value of investments for which there is no available market;

6.14.22.4 The effect of contractual terms and their commercial consequences (again this is good news for lawyers);

6.14.22.5 How to structure a transaction to comply with regulatory, competition or taxation requirements; or

6.14.22.6 Terms which are commonly accepted in the market.

6.14.23 As a result of the helpful guidance in PERG 8, it is generally possible for clients to avoid the provision of regulated investment advice (if they wish to do so) by ensuring they restrict their services to the provision of information only.

6.14.24 Exclusions

6.14.24.1 The following general exclusions apply to the advising activity. As before, the asterix suggests that the exclusion is not available in relation to the activities which are carried on by MiFID investment firms:

(a) Acting as trustee;

(b) Carrying on a profession or business;*

(c) Sale of goods or services;*

(d) Group exclusion;*

(e) Sale of body corporate;*

(f) Overseas persons.

6.15 Agreeing (Article 64 RAO)

6.15.1 It is also important to bear in mind (and PERG reminds us at PERG 2.7.21 G) that agreeing to carry on most regulated activities is in itself a regulated activity (although that is not always the case, for example if the underlying activities relate to accepting deposits, effecting or carrying out contracts of insurance, managing a UCITS or AIF or acting as trustee or depositary of one, among others).

6.15.2 The overseas persons exclusion applies in part where a person agrees to carry on a regulated activity and the agreement is reached as a result of a legitimate approach (PERG 2.8.15 G), but only if the agreement is one to arrange deals, manage investments or safeguard and administer investments.

6.16 The General Exclusions

The following General Exclusions are the most broadly used:

6.16.1 Trustees, nominees and personal representatives (Article 66 RAO)

6.16.1.1 PERG confirms at PERG 2.9.4 G that if a person is acting in a representative capacity they may not need to be authorised.

6.16.1.2 Many of the exclusions are linked into the general discharge of trustee or representative obligations when acting in that role.

6.16.1.3 They generally require the trustee or representative not to hold themselves out as providing the services that consist of the relevant regulated activity.

6.16.1.4 The trustee or representative must also not receive remuneration that is additional to any that they receive when acting in that role. PERG confirms here that a person will not be deemed to be receiving additional remuneration merely because this remuneration is calculated by reference to time spent.

6.16.2 Professions or business not involving regulated activities (Article 67 RAO)

6.16.2.1 PERG 2.9.6 G confirms that this exclusion applies where the activity is carried on in the course of a profession or business which does not otherwise consist of the carrying on of regulated activities in the UK. However, the activities are only able to be excluded if they can "reasonably be regarded" as a necessary part of the other services provided in the course of the profession or business.

6.16.2.2 If the services are separately remunerated then the exclusion won't apply (see PERG 2.9.6 G).

6.16.2.3 When combined with the "not by way of business" argument, this can be a very helpful exclusionfor businesses that carry on regulated activities that are incidental to the services that represent the main part of the business that is carried on.

6.16.2.4 Law firm partners often become concerned that they may be carrying on regulated activities (and indeed I have been asked to advise on this issue several times!), but the argument is that any such activities may be incidental to the ordinary activity of acting as a solicitor.

6.16.2.5 This exclusion is disapplied for persons who are MiFID investment firms.

6.16.3 Sale of goods and supply of services (Article 68 RAO)

6.16.3.1 PERG 2.9.8 G confirms that these exclusions focus on where the main business is to sell goods or supply services, but where certain activities may have to be carried on for the purposes of that business, which may otherwise be regulated activities.

6.16.3.2 They will not be available if the customer to whom goods or services are sold is an individual.

6.16.3.3 They are also disapplied if the person carrying on the activity is a MiFID investment firm.

6.16.4 The group exclusion (Article 69 RAO)

6.16.4.1 The group exclusion is potentially a very useful option when entities are providing services to other entities within their corporate group. For example, an investment advisory entity onshore in the UK may be providing investment advice to a US company in its group. If structured correctly, the activities of the UK entity will be excluded from being regulated. The exclusion applies (amongst others) to the regulated activities of dealing as agent, arranging, managing investments and advising on investments.

6.16.4.2 PERG 2.9.10 G advises that these exclusions apply to intra-group dealings and activities. Further, PERG confirms that the general principle is that as long as activities that would be regulated activities take place within a group of companies, there is no need for authorisation.

6.16.4.3 The group exclusion is subject to the MiFID override. What this means is that if a MiFID investment firm wants to make use of the group exclusion, then the narrower MiFID definition of group applies.

6.16.4.4 If non-MiFID, the concept of a participating interest exists, PERG confirms here that this means that dealings or activities involving participators in a joint enterprise (which take place for the purposes of that enterprise) will also be excluded. The term joint enterprise is defined at Article 3(1) of the RAO as an enterprise into which two or more persons enter for commercial purposes related to a business carried on by them. Where a participator is a member of a group, each other member of the group is also to be regarded as a participator in the enterprise.

6.16.4.5 The MiFID definition means that on a strict interpretation investment services within the scope of MiFID may only be provided to a parent, subsidiary or sister company.

6.16.5 Sale of body corporate (Article 70 RAO)

6.16.5.1 This exclusion relates to selling companies, the effect of which is to avoid merger and acquisition type transactions looking like the carrying on of regulated activities requiring authorisation from the FCA as a result.

6.16.5.2 The exclusion covers the types of activities that would ordinarily be carried on in a corporate transaction such as dealing, arranging and advising.

6.16.5.3 PERG 2.9.12 G confirms that the exclusion applies in relation to transactions to buy or sell shares in a body corporate (note, this does not cover the shares of an open-ended investment company, which would be viewed as a fund vehicle) where:

(a) The transaction involves the acquisition or disposal of at least 50 per cent of the voting shares in the body corporate and is, or is to be, between certain specified kinds of person;

(b) The object of the transaction may otherwise reasonably be regarded as being the acquisition of day-to-day control of the affairs of the body corporate.

6.16.5.4 The exclusion is disapplied for MiFID investment firms.

6.16.5.5 Thus, if an entity is carrying on "corporate finance business" as a professional services business, then they should seek regulation rather than relying on this exclusion.

6.16.5.6 Further, it is important to note that this exclusion is for acquisitions relating to 50% or more of voting power or control. Where a person is carrying on the above-mentioned regulated activities that might otherwise be excluded under this definition, these will not be available if investors are taking minority stakes.

6.16.6 Employee share schemes (Article 71 RAO)

6.16.6.1 PERG 2.9.14 G confirms that this exclusion in broad terms applies to activities which further an employee share scheme or are carried on in its operation; they apply to activities carried on by the company whose securities or debentures (which term has an extended meaning here) are the subject of the scheme.

6.16.6.2 PERG highlights that the exclusion also applies to activities of a company in the same group of a trustee who holds securities or debentures under the scheme but not to the activities of a person who is not such a company or trustee (for example, a third-party administration provider). The meaning of group is wider than the company law definition.

6.16.7 Overseas persons (Article 72 RAO)

6.16.7.1 PERG 2.9.16 G tells us that an overseas person is a person who carries on what would be regulated activities but who does not do so, or offer to do so, from a permanent place of business maintained by him in the UK.

6.16.7.2 Certain offshore entities, including large offshore private banks, rely heavily on the overseas persons exclusion to provide services cross border into the UK.

6.16.7.3 The exclusion allows the overseas person to enter into deals on behalf of a person in the UK or give them advice.

6.16.7.4 Where they do not have a permanent place of business in the UK, they will not need to rely on the exclusion unless what they do is regarded as carried on in the UK (PERG 2.4 covers this).

6.16.7.5 There are broadly speaking two categories of activities covered under the overseas persons exclusion:

(a) The first is where the regulated activity requires the direct involvement of another person and that person is authorised or exempt (and acting within the scope of his exemption). PERG gives the example of the overseas person dealing with an authorised person and the arrangements being for transactions to be entered by such a person.

(b) The second and more useful option is where the regulated activity is carried on as a result of what is deemed a "legitimate approach". It is this limb that tends to be relied upon by overseas persons approaching the UK.

6.16.7.6 A "legitimate approach" is an approach to an overseas person that has not been solicited by him in any way, or has been solicited in a way that does not contravene the Financial Promotion Restriction. Crucially, PERG provides that an approach that is *made by the overseas person* that does not contravene the Financial Promotion Restriction is also a legitimate approach.

6.16.7.7 The way that offshore financial services firm normally use the overseas person exclusion is that they will approach a UK based person using one of the financial promotion exemptions in the FPO and go from there.

6.16.7.8 So if an overseas person approaches a UK person using a relevant exemption set out in the FPO, this will deemed to have resulted from a "legitimate approach".

6.16.7.9 Further, the UK Government is generally accepting of offshore firms relying on it in an effort to encourage business into the UK. Several years ago there was talk of consulting on the application of the exclusion, but I am not aware that the proposals have been picked up again.

6.16.7.10 Note that the overseas persons exclusion is also available in relation to home finance transactions, but that they apply depending on the residence of the borrower (and link into whether there is a sufficient "UK nexus"). As these are specialist regimes they are outside the scope of this manual, but information can be found in PERG 4.11 and PERG 14.6.

CHAPTER SEVEN

CONCLUSIONS

7.1 I hope this guide is helpful as an introduction to the general concepts of the UK regulatory regime. You will see that it only scratches the surface of a regime that is complicated and overlayed with various pieces of European legislation.

7.2 You will have been introduced to the regulated activities regime as a whole and have been made aware of the relevant exclusions and exemptions that apply, as well as guidance in PERG that is useful to considering whether those activities are being carried on. This guide has also introduced concepts such as financial promotions and MiFID.

7.3 It is my understanding that the current UK Government intends to overhaul elements of the regulatory regime in an effort to make it easier for firms to do business and with an overall aim of achieving growth. At the date of writing, there are consultations on changing various elements of the regulatory regime, for example simplifying the regime relating to consumer credit (which this guide has only touched on briefly, given its intricacies!).

7.4 It can only be the case that simplifying the web of legislation is welcome. I look forward to seeing how the regime develops and is (hopefully) streamlined over time. But in the meantime, you have this guide to aid in your interpretation!

MORE BOOKS BY LAW BRIEF PUBLISHING

A selection of our other titles available now:-

'A Practical Guide to Probation Breaches and Other Applications' by Mark Thomas
'A Practical Guide to Remarriage and Divorce' by Cordelia Williams & Claire Howard
'A Practical Guide to Privacy, Transparency, Reporting Restrictions and Closed Proceedings in the Court of Protection' by Laura Mannering
'Beaumont on Barristers – A Guide to Defending Disciplinary Proceedings (Second Edition)' by Marc Beaumont
'A Practical Guide to Payments for Environmental Services' by Ben Sharples
'A Practical Guide to the Law of Pregnancy and Maternity at Work' by Rebecca Thomas
'A Practical Guide to Redundancy – Second Edition' by Philip Hyland & Collette Moore
'A Practical Guide to International Issues for Scottish Family Lawyers' by Susie Mountain, Donna McKay, Ken MacDonald
'A Practical Guide to the Law on Deprivation of Liberty' by Ben Troke
'A Practical Guide to Rights over Airspace and Subsoil – Second Edition' by Daniel Gatty
'A Practical Guide to the Law in Relation to Inquests' by Ramya Nagesh
'A Practical Guide to the Construction and Rectification of Wills and Trust Instruments (Second Edition)' by Edward Hewitt
'A Practical Guide to Data Protection in Social Housing' by Clare Paterson
'A Practical Guide to Spousal Maintenance – Second Edition' by Liz Cowell
'A Practical Guide to International Parental Child Abduction Law (England and Wales)' by Dr Onyója Momoh
'A Practical Guide to Deprivation of British Citizenship' by Sean Ell
'A Practical Guide to Commercial Property Service Charges' by Rachel Garton
'A Practical Guide to Clinical Negligence – Third Edition' by Geoffrey Simpson-Scott (Geoff)
'A Practical Guide to the Rights of Grandparents in Children Proceedings – Second Edition' by Stuart Barlow

'The Electronic Communications Code: A Practical Guide – Second Edition' by Kerry Bretherton KC, James Castle, Mark Loveday
'A Practical Guide to the Independent School Standards – September 2023 Edition' by Sarah McKimm
'A Practical Guide to Estate Administration and Crypto Assets' by Richard Marshall
'A Practical Guide to Parental Alienation in Private and Public Law Children Cases' by Sam King QC & Frankie Shama
'Contested Heritage – Removing Art from Land and Historic Buildings' by Richard Harwood QC, Catherine Dobson, David Sawtell
'The Limits of Separate Legal Personality: When Those Running a Company Can Be Held Personally Liable for Losses Caused to Third Parties Outside of the Company' by Dr Mike Wilkinson
'A Practical Guide to Transgender Law' by Robin Moira White & Nicola Newbegin
'A Practical Guide to 'Stranded Spouses' in Family Law' by Mani Singh Basi
'A Practical Guide to Residential Freehold Conveyancing' by Lorraine Richardson
'A Practical Guide to Pensions on Divorce for Lawyers' by Bryan Scant
'A Practical Guide to Challenging Sham Marriage Allegations in Immigration Law' by Priya Solanki
'A Practical Guide to Digital Communications Evidence in Criminal Law' by Sam Willis
'A Practical Guide to Legal Rights in Scotland' by Sarah-Jane Macdonald
'A Practical Guide to New Build Conveyancing' by Paul Sams & Rebecca East
'A Practical Guide to Inherited Wealth on Divorce' by Hayley Trim
'A Practical Guide to Practice Direction 12J and Domestic Abuse in Private Law Children Proceedings' by Rebecca Cross & Malvika Jaganmohan
'A Practical Guide to Confiscation and Restraint' by Narita Bahra QC, John Carl Townsend, David Winch
'A Practical Guide to the Law of Forests in Scotland' by Philip Buchan
'A Practical Guide to Health and Medical Cases in Immigration Law' by Rebecca Chapman & Miranda Butler
'A Practical Guide to Bad Character Evidence for Criminal Practitioners by Aparna Rao
'A Practical Guide to Extradition Law post-Brexit' by Myles Grandison et al
'A Practical Guide to Hoarding and Mental Health for Housing Lawyers' by Rachel Coyle

'Stephens on Contractual Indemnities' by Richard Stephens
'A Practical Guide to the EU Succession Regulation' by Richard Frimston
'A Practical Guide to Solicitor and Client Costs – Second Edition' by Robin Dunne
'Constructive Dismissal – Practice Pointers and Principles' by Benjimin Burgher
'A Practical Guide to Religion and Belief Discrimination Claims in the Workplace' by Kashif Ali
'A Practical Guide to the Law of Medical Treatment Decisions' by Ben Troke
'Fundamental Dishonesty and QOCS in Personal Injury Proceedings: Law and Practice' by Jake Rowley
'A Practical Guide to the Law in Relation to School Exclusions' by Charlotte Hadfield & Alice de Coverley
'A Practical Guide to Divorce for the Silver Separators' by Karin Walker
'The Right to be Forgotten – The Law and Practical Issues' by Melissa Stock
'A Practical Guide to Planning Law and Rights of Way in National Parks, the Broads and AONBs' by James Maurici QC, James Neill et al
'A Practical Guide to Election Law' by Tom Tabori
'A Practical Guide to the Law in Relation to Surrogacy' by Andrew Powell
'A Practical Guide to Claims Arising from Fatal Accidents – Second Edition' by James Patience
'A Practical Guide to Asbestos Claims' by Jonathan Owen & Gareth McAloon
'A Practical Guide to Stamp Duty Land Tax in England and Northern Ireland' by Suzanne O'Hara
'A Practical Guide to the Law of Farming Partnerships' by Philip Whitcomb
'A Practical Guide to the Law of Unlawful Eviction and Harassment – Second Edition' by Stephanie Lovegrove
'A Practical Guide to Costs in Personal Injury Claims – Second Edition' by Matthew Hoe
'A Practical Guide to the General Data Protection Regulation (GDPR) – Second Edition' by Keith Markham
'A Practical Guide to Working with Litigants in Person and McKenzie Friends in Family Cases' by Stuart Barlow
'Protecting Unregistered Brands: A Practical Guide to the Law of Passing Off' by Lorna Brazell
'A Practical Guide to Secondary Liability and Joint Enterprise Post-Jogee' by Joanne Cecil & James Mehigan

'A Practical Guide to the Pre-Action RTA Claims Protocol for Personal Injury Lawyers' by Antonia Ford
'A Practical Guide to Neighbour Disputes and the Law' by Alexander Walsh
'A Practical Guide to Coercive Control for Legal Practitioners and Victims' by Rachel Horman
'A Practical Guide to the Law of Driverless Cars – Second Edition'
by Alex Glassbrook, Emma Northey & Scarlett Milligan
'A Practical Guide to TOLATA Claims' by Greg Williams
'A Practical Guide to Elderly Law – Second Edition' by Justin Patten
'A Practical Guide to Responding to Housing Disrepair and Unfitness Claims' by Iain Wightwick
'A Practical Guide to the Law of Bullying and Harassment in the Workplace' by Philip Hyland
'How to Be a Freelance Solicitor: A Practical Guide to the SRA-Regulated Freelance Solicitor Model' by Paul Bennett
'A Practical Guide to Prison Injury Claims' by Malcolm Johnson
'A Practical Guide to Advising Clients at the Police Station' by Colin Stephen McKeown-Beaumont
'A Practical Guide to Antisocial Behaviour Injunctions – Second Edition' by Iain Wightwick
'Practical Mediation: A Guide for Mediators, Advocates, Advisers, Lawyers, and Students in Civil, Commercial, Business, Property, Workplace, and Employment Cases' by Jonathan Dingle with John Sephton
'The Mini-Pupillage Workbook' by David Boyle
'A Practical Guide to Crofting Law' by Brian Inkster
'A Practical Guide to the Law of Domain Names and Cybersquatting' by Andrew Clemson
'A Practical Guide to the Law of Gender Pay Gap Reporting' by Harini Iyengar
'NHS Whistleblowing and the Law' by Joseph England
'Employment Law and the Gig Economy' by Nigel Mackay & Annie Powell
'A Practical Guide to Noise Induced Hearing Loss (NIHL) Claims' by Andrew Mckie, Ian Skeate, Gareth McAloon
'An Introduction to Beauty Negligence Claims – A Practical Guide for the Personal Injury Practitioner' by Greg Almond
'Intercompany Agreements for Transfer Pricing Compliance' by Paul Sutton
'Zen and the Art of Mediation' by Martin Plowman
'A Practical Guide to Adoption for Family Lawyers' by Graham Pegg

'A Practical Guide to Industrial Disease Claims' by Andrew Mckie & Ian Skeate
'A Practical Guide to Conducting a Sheriff Court Proof' by Andrew Stevenson
'A Practical Guide to Vicarious Liability' by Mariel Irvine
'A Practical Guide to Applications for Landlord's Consent and Variation of Leases' by Mark Shelton
'A Practical Guide to Relief from Sanctions Post-Mitchell and Denton' by Peter Causton
'A Practical Guide to Equity Release for Advisors' by Paul Sams
'A Practical Guide to Financial Services Claims' by Chris Hegarty
'A Practical Guide to Financial Ombudsman Service Claims' by Adam Temple & Robert Scrivenor
'A Practical Guide to Running Housing Disrepair and Cavity Wall Claims – Second Edition' by Andrew Mckie & Ian Skeate
'A Practical Guide to Holiday Sickness Claims – Second Edition' by Andrew Mckie & Ian Skeate
'Arguments and Tactics for Personal Injury and Clinical Negligence Claims' by Dorian Williams
'A Practical Guide to Drone Law' by Rufus Ballaster, Andrew Firman, Eleanor Clot
'On Experts: CPR35 for Lawyers and Experts' by David Boyle
'An Introduction to Personal Injury Law' by David Boyle

These books and more are available to order online direct from the publisher at www.lawbriefpublishing.com, where you can also read free sample chapters. For any queries, call us on 0844 587 2383 or email us at mail@lawbriefpublishing.com.

Our books are all generally in stock at www.amazon.co.uk with free next day delivery for Prime members, and at good legal bookshops such as Wildy & Sons.

We are regularly launching new books in our series of practical day-to-day practitioners' guides. Visit our website and join our free newsletter to be kept informed and to receive special offers, free chapters, etc.

You can also follow us on Twitter at www.twitter.com/lawbriefpub.

www.ingramcontent.com/pod-product-compliance
Ingram Content Group UK Ltd.
Pitfield, Milton Keynes, MK11 3LW, UK
UKHW020149290926
15471UKWH00004B/779

9 781916 698956